"THINK AND WRITE IN INK"

'TRAIN YOUR BRAIN TO EARN GRAIN'

PONNADA NAGA SURENDRA

I dedicate this book to my family and friends. A gratitude and special thanks to "**SiTaRa**" for standing beside me and inspiring in an odd time.

I dedicate this book to my adorable friends who helped me through out the process. Your ideas, guidance and motivation always helped me in reaching my destination with few hurdles.

last but not the least,

I would like to dedicate this book to the readers who supported my first book "**I DEAL IDEAS**". Your suggestions helped me alot in updating and sorting out the mistakes in my book.

Contents

Preface

"The main purpose of publishing this book is not for seeking any praise from somebody or to become popular. There are many readers in our country and the states who like to read those books written by their favourite authors. My solely hope is that, I want authors to write a book and publish it in the name of an old age home or orphanage account. Need to see, when the book is taken by someone then the money should be deposited directly in the orphanage's bank account. If your book sells more than the expected then there is no need for that orphanage or nursing home to wait for funds. Taking this as an initiative, I am publishing this book in the name of an organisation. A good book can increase a person's life moments."

With regards,

Enter Caption

Acknowledgements

"I have to start by thanking my friends, colleagues and my parents. From going through early drafts and giving me the advice on the cover. so I could edit and present it before you. Thank you so much. I would not be in this position if you did not influence and motivate me."

CHAPTER ONE

DUST PARTICLES

Introduction :-

" "Yes, Dust particles may be abiotic Lilliputs in our life but we should not have to be Gulliver in their life." "

Do you know how the dust particles create a minute impact on us?

If not !! then we will discuss.

Whenever we go to a new place, the first thing that we notice is the physical properties of that area.

1. We catch the scenic beauty of that area with our eyes.
2. We touch the existing plants and materials in the surrounding areas.
3. We could smell the Fragrances of flowers, the scent of the soil or any other materials with our noses.
4. We can hear birds chirping, rustling made by leaves and river babbling with our ears.

But the most important thing is a sense of feeling!! We can feel the temperature of that area that how cool the temperature is, how hot and mild, how humidity and other thermal properties with our senses.

"But why all these senses are needed in this topic?" That might be your question.

Topic:-

In this context, I am going to talk over one of the minute problems that are being not considered by us in our daily life and later on, which may sometimes lead to heavy destruction.

Plant species in some Places like INDIA, Africa and some other countries are often damaged due to dust particles in their vicinity.

But how?

Before knowing about how it is affecting, we have to know some details regarding dust particles. **Dust particles** are minute particles which are present on the land surface formed due to crushing stones and from residual products in thermal stations which are having a size ranging from 1 µm to 100 µm. They are having very small gravity, as a result, these dust particles are being lifted up easily by air molecules. These are sometimes referred to as sediments with negligible gravity. when heavy wind outpours from one area to another it carries those sediment particles with it.

Stoma or stomata

Let us know about **stoma or stomata** which means a small hole which is having a diameter ranging from 11 µm-80µm some of them are even smaller than 60 µm. These stomas are present in millions on leaves. So, the question is how do dust particles are emerging as damage to trees or plants?

"Due to the swift movement of vehicles on roads, air acts as a medium and lifts the particles into the atmosphere which are completely negligible to gravity. After a time gap, these particles start falling on the ground surface and some of them even get Deposited on the leaves of plants that are present along the road. The main function of the stroma is the transpiration process we know that out of 100% of water plants use only 4%-5% of water for their basic needs and the remaining water is being sent to the atmosphere with the help of this stroma by the process of transpiration."

$$6CO_2 + 12H_2O \xrightarrow[\text{green plants}]{\text{light}} C_6H_{12}O_6 + 6O_2 + 6H_2O.$$

carbon dioxide   water   glucose   oxygen   water

PHOTOSYNTHESIS

What is the use of transpiration?

The air usually moves from high pressure to low pressure. when moving from high pressure it carries small water droplets that are present on leaves with it and transport them to other areas, as a result, we could sense cool fresh air when we sit under a tree or its vicinity.

Due to the fast-moving of vehicles, a mammoth amount of dust particles is lifted and deposited on the leaves erupting the transpiration process as a result transpiration process is very low compares to other places sometimes plants may succumb as dust particles blocks transpiration process.

Hence, the air that is present around these areas is very hot as water molecules are not being able to transport.

CASE 1:-

why it only be water?

"can't air transport dust that is present on leaves?"

Yes, it will transport but some dust particles fit into the size of a stoma and don't get easily transported.

It causes uncomfortable life in those areas. Even the oxygen levels decrease due to less number of plants and the photosynthesis process. There are of the minute form.

CASE 2:-

Then what about other soil particles like humus, sand, coarse and fine aggregate.

Humus: -

Humus is an organic material that is formed due to decomposing of dead leaves and organic material and hence these posses very small size to maximum size.

Conditions that may happens when humus is deposited

1. Getting deposited in to pores and blocks water but humus absorbs water and hence binding nature can be easily destroyed and hence humus impact on transpiration is very less.
2. How humus reacts with leaves? as humus mainly of dead and organic material the impacts and reaction might is negligible.

Sand and other aggregate:

Sand and coarse aggregates are of different sizes.it may vary from 4.75 µm in fine aggregate to 60-70cm large boulders.

There are two main important properties which play an important role

1. Gravity: most of the particles not lifted up due to gravity. Even, if they got lifted and deposited on leaves, these particles won't withstand in pores or on leaves. Gradually falls downward.
2. Adsorption: it is one of the most important things which is closely related to absorption. Former, where particles water particles are accumulated around the substances and later, the water particles are taken into by the substances.

Hence, because of gravity and adsorption, the effect on transpiration is very less. But the adsorption of smaller particles or fine particles that are accumulated on leaves play a minute impacts. In this study we are neglecting this property.

Experimental study:
Required:- Leaf, chalk Powder, Flash light.

Enter Caption

Procedure:-

1. Initially take a leaf and place it under a flash light.

    Case 1:- As stoma size is very minute the shadow that is formed is dark colour.

1. To make it more feasible make small holes on leaves with pencil and place it under a flash light. Now, we can see small holes on shadow through which light is passed.

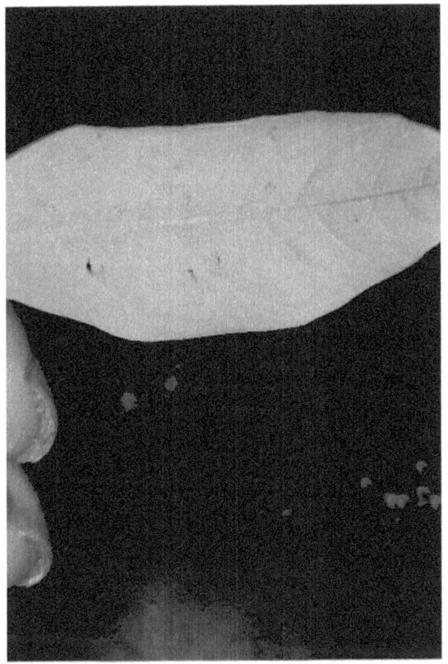

LEAF WITH VOIDS

3. Now, considering powder as silt and deposited on leaves.

SILT DEPOSITION

Initially, silt deposited on leaf less amounts less even in those conditions we can see light passes through holes. Again we have deposited powder on leaf by increasing its quantity. Now, holes are slowly getting blocked.

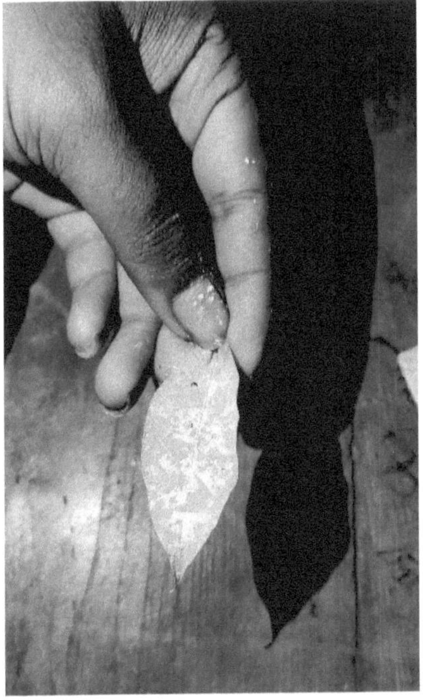

LEAF WITH BLOCKED VOIDS

Constant accumulation of silt on leaves not only blocks sunlight but also rapid decrease in transpiration process.

4. Now considering other seasonal aspects like rain in rainy season and moisture in winter season. Now, chalk powder is made into a paste and painted on leaf (considering as mud) left for some time then the paste got dried up and don't allowed light to pass through it if the accumulation is more on leaves. Same thing happens in moisture condition also.

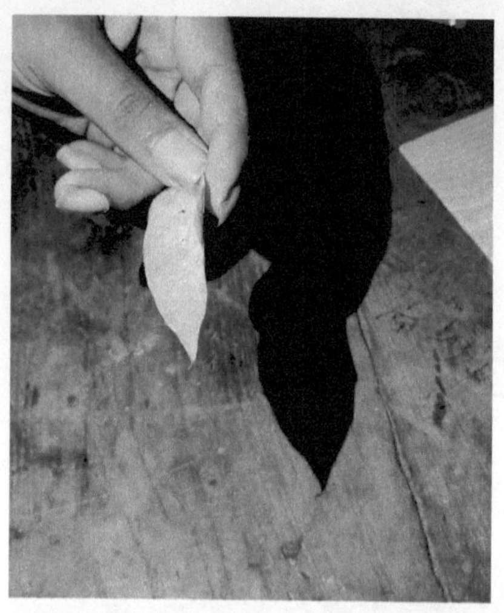

SLURRY DEPOSITION IN RAINY SEASON

Impacts due to this process:

- Transpiration rate gradually decreases on a minute scale and sometimes in the negligible form
- If the rate of transpiration decreases plants and leaves cells are filled with water molecules and it shrinks very fast.
- If leaves decreases then there will be a change in the photosynthesis process.
- Hence, there will be an increase in temperature in that area.
- These dust particles do not even allow any light as light plays a major role in photosynthesis.
- All the above conditions happen on a minute scale. Considering those facts are always secondary.

Where can we see maximum accumulation?

1. Quarrying
2. Mining
3. Thermal industries
4. Carpentry
5. Industries etc ....

In all the above cases we can see max accumulation of silt on leaves and as a result and leaves that are present near its vicinity looks white in colour.

Steps to stop this effect:

* Make sure land is not filled with soil particles or dust particles. If so, regular maintenance should be done 'Water should be sprinkled daily to stop dust from depositing on leaves
* Cargo which is carrying minute particles like sand or coal or crushed stone materials should be covered to make sure all the dust particles should not get lifted
* Growing as many numbers of trees so as to ebb the temperature of the nascent area.

For more understanding, we can take an example

"Have you ever observed why the colour of houses beside a road fade away?"

Due to the fast movement of vehicles, the particles are lifted up and at a certain time those mud particles get deposited on the walls of the houses that are present beside that road and leading to a scary look and fading out the scenic beauty of that house externally

To avoid all these problems some companies are using

some types of emulsions and varnishes to stop dust particles from being deposited on these walls.

Conclusion :-

Eventually, we may think we are doing very less harm by throwing or leaving dust particles maybe one day these particles going to create a big impact on you and your surroundings.

Hope you understand this concept.

> *""BELIEVE ME, EVEN IN BIG BANG THEORY THE PARTICLES ARE OF VERY MINUTE BUT EVOLUTION LEADS TO A HUMONGOUS AREA.""*

Our Environment and Our life. we should protect that..

" "

CHAPTER TWO

MYTH or SCIENCE

""MYTH IS A MEANINGFUL WORD WHICH STUDIES PAST CULTURE WHEREAS SCIENCE IS A SCIENTIFIC WORD WHICH DETECTS MYTH. ONE CAN ONLY DETECT IF HE STUDIES WELL.""

These are like 2 sides to a coin very difficult to predict and demonstrate.

"Have you detected floating stones?"

This subject is a combination of Mythology and Science.

Let us first discuss the **mythological** purpose of reading. "In Ramayana, Sita, the wife of Rama was absconded by Ravana to his kingdom. Once crossing all hurdles and barriers Rama came to grasp Sita was present in the kingdom of Ravana. However, he had to cross Saptha Samudra to reach Ravana's kingdom. So, he prayed to Samudra deva, the ocean god and he gave him a boon that if Rama or his soldiers throw something into the sea, he would build them to float on the ocean. As a result, Rama could be able to build Ramasethu (Adams bridge) and cross all along Saptha Samudra and fight with Ravana and save Sita."

The mythological student believes that this would have happened. however, science student always seeks of knowing how stones in that space are able to float. Even with the help of satellite images, the vandalized Adams bridge was clearly seen. But most of the theories regarding this weren't in the least approved. Some assumptions regarding this made me think out of the box.

According to **science**:-

The main important concept that is present in this is density. As we all know that density is the mass per unit volume. If the density is more it remains underwater if not it floats on water. Since water has a density of 1kg/cubic M. Materials above 1 remain underwater and below 1 float on water.

The density of stone is bigger than water as a result stones don't float in water but coming to Adams bridge, in most of the journals it was clearly mentioned, that Pumice and other volcanic rocks end in floating of stones in water.

But the question is how?

Before discussing, however, we tend to stumble upon, what are the different types of rocks.

Rocks are classified into three types

1. Igneous.

2. Sedimentary.

3. Metamorphic rocks.

Igneous rocks: Igneous rocks are formed due to the rapid cooling of lava which is erupted from the volcano. These rocks contain small pores on their surfaces and all these pores are filled with air and thence these are lightweight in density.

eg: Basalt, Granite etc.

Usually, pumice rock comes under the sedimentary

category.

Sedimentary rocks: Rocks formed due to sediments or tiny particles these stones are also lightweight and are having less density.

   eg:- Sandstone, Limestone, etc

Metamorphic rock: These rocks are formed due to changes in temperature and pressure.

   eg:- Marble, Quartzite etc.

   "ANSWERS CAN BE SEIZED ONLY WHEN QUESTIONS ARE TOSSED."

Now the questions are
1. How do they(Rama and soldiers) know this rock floats in water?
2. Is there any evidence to prove the presence of pumice rock in Tamil Nadu?
3. Is there any volcanic eruptions during that period?
4. What material was used for the binding of rocks?
5. Whether the bridge is constructed in shallow depth or deep?

There are the main questions that needed to be answered by the science student.

Let us make some assumptions to answer these questions.
1. Weight of the stone clearly gives us how stone acts in the water. If the weight of the stone is high it sinks quickly. Only if that sea has high salinity, rocks can be able to float. Hence, this condition is to be considered.
2. Length of the bridge is nearly 4 km. can rock having the same characteristic properties exist throughout the bridge

but it's practically not possible to find the same stone from all different types of rocks and Stones. It would be possible only if there was a pumice mountain in that area.

3. As per seismological data there are very a much smaller number of active volcanoes in a place like Rameswaram in Tamil nada then how do they get volcanic rocks for a length of nearly 4 km.

4. Rocks don't seem to be having similar shapes hence different rocks possess different shapes as a result the gaps that are present in between layers are being filled with other rocks.

5. *Case 1*:- Depth

If the depth of area increases the number of stones conjointly will increases as a result we would have found many rocks in that area.

Case 2:- shallow depth

if it is a shallow depth we would have found the constant deposition as the bridge act as a barrier for the movement of sand that is present in that area. As a result, heavy deposition of sand takes place.

This topic will come to an end only when we have specific data regarding that area, carbon dating details, and topographic features of that area.

I will come to the end that this topic is somewhat troublesome to understand and analyse some questions can't be answered without having clear data.

How rock transforms when it presents in the water

Rocks undergo weathering it may be leeching, hydrolysis, carbonation, or oxidation.

In my study, I came to know leeching of stones and sedimentation took place, as a result, most of the stones sink in water and because of high tides there end up in crushing of those stones and hence we can't find a large number of stones in that area.

In the 2004 tsunami in the Indian ocean, some floating stones came to shore near the Tamilnadu area.

If you would like to grasp details about floating stones you can refer to floating stones in Rameswaram on YouTube.

NEXT QUESTION IS
ONE OF MY FRIENDS HAS THROWN THIS QUESTION AT ME.

"Does Rama really exist?"

It's a bit hypothetical question but I will strive my best to make u perceive it clearly. we all knew zero degrees is called an EQUATOR. Taking the equator as a reference we will find locations, longitudinal and latitudinal ranges. Just like the same thing, Rama is like an equator in humans with the help of his attitude, and behaviour we will be ready to abide by nice nature and solve all sorts of problems. If u believe Rama is a god you will positively assume god has some supernatural powers and hence we don't show any interest to follow but if we believe Rama as an IDEAL man we will try our best to be like Rama.

> *""WE DON'T HAVE THE POWER TO MANIPULATE MYTHOLOGY BUT AT THE SAME TIME WE HAVE LESS INTELLIGENCE TO DECODE THE SCIENTIFIC REASONS BEHIND A MYTH."*
> *"*

CHAPTER THREE

LIGHT POLLUTION

*"**"I don't know whether the light has weight but this content does have!!!!!"***

"Have you heard about light pollution?"

Well, most people have not come across this word.

The majority of people in rural and urban areas are somehow directly or indirectly responsible for this act.

let's talk briefly about pollution.

From our childhood days, we have learned many things about pollution. Based on their impinging, There are different types of pollution in our environment.

They are as follows:

1. Air pollution
2. Water pollution.
3. Land pollution

These are the main categories of pollution. Besides these, there are also many other types of pollution like Light pollution, Thermal pollution, Nuclear reactors' pollution etc.

Although light pollution, thermal pollution, and nuclear pollution are not considered primary pollution, the impacts caused by these are very high.

In this topic, I would like to discuss Light pollution

Most people are not much aware of light pollution but light pollution endangered the lives of many Nocturnal animals and was also responsible for negative effects on human beings.

Before discussing light pollution and its impacts, we should be aware of the difference between Nocturnal and Diurnal animals.

Nocturnal animals:- These may be defined as the animals which work during the night time in searching for food, moving from place to place for habitation and escaping from predators and sleeping during the day time these are defined as the Nocturnal animals

e.g:- Fox, Dog, Owl, Bats etc.

Diurnal animals:- Animals which work during day time and sleep during nighttime are defined as diurnal animals

e.g:- Buffalo, Cow, Goats, Man etc.

Light pollution is caused due to the unnecessary and excessive usage of lights which may lead to the death of several nocturnal animals and also human beings. Disrupts the eyesight of animals and people who are driving.

"But the question is how?"

Usually, nocturnal animals roam around the vicinity and nascent areas in search of food and other requirements but the lights that are present which are used by the humans in commercial or street lights or any other distracts the way of the animals and finally leads to the collision to houses or electrical poles nearby which ultimately succumb to that death of that nocturnal animals.

As per reports the population of fox, wolf, and owls get endangered. One of the factors that lead to the decline of the fox is light pollution

let me tell you a brief example of how these nocturnal animals live during the daytime or if excess usage of light during nighttime.

We know that a Bat is the only mammal that can fly from one area to another. During the nighttime, it's very easy for a bat to travel and catch food. Usually bat travel from one place to another using infrasonic waves, which means sound waves with a frequency less than 20Hz that human beings can't hear. Echoes act an important role in their travelling

when the bat moves it produces infrasonic waves if there is any object or building present the echoes get transmitted back and give a signal to the bat and then the bat escapes from these hurdles. That is why bats in daytime stagger. But coming to light pollution, it is completely different compared to others. Bats are being distracted by the light rays hence bats don't find a clear path to travel as a result they get collide with moving vehicles or any other building eventually leading to fatalities. Other animals also move during the night to gather food and hunt predators.

"Nocturnal animals are not from space but they are seeking some space on earth."

Impacts on human beings

1. Eye problems.
2. Insomnia.

3. Distraction during driving.
4. Health problems based on the intensity of light.

Ways to decrease light pollution

1. Extra usage and unnecessary usage of lights should be prevented.
2. Should create awareness among people.
3. Should protect those species which are getting endangered.
4. Street lights should be turned off after 10 PM, if not necessary and for safety, we can use a CC camera having night vision.
5. Nocturnal animal areas should be discovered and danger signboards should be provided.
6. Light which affects less on animals and emits a good amount should be used.

"We can't divert light's path but we can turn off that."

Eventually, I would like to say this earth is not only for human beings to live it is also for all other species on this earth it's our responsibility to protect them and save them. They don't need our sympathy they need our concern to help them and save them.

""Yes, I can't segregate light but I can aggregate humans to fight against light pollution.""

CHAPTER FOUR

AIR CONDITIONING

"Do you know what will happen, if air conditioning and fan are used at the same time?"

As we knew that air conditioning was used either to decrease the surrounding high temperature or to increase, during summer and winter.

Hence, there will be three cases if both air conditioning and fan are used at the same time.

- The room temperature decreases.
- Increases.
- Remains unaltered.

I will give you an awfully simple idea regarding this subject.

We know that matter exists in 3 main forms

1. Solids.
2. Liquids.
3. Gases.

The other two forms are plasma and the Bose-Einstein model.

SOLIDS:-

In solids, the particles are closely packed. Hence, we can neglect this state. Solids require or intake most energy to interrupt the attraction forces. So most people will not suggest you put AC wherever utensils, racks, and gunny bags are present.

LIQUIDS:-
In liquids, the particles are not closely packed and hence we are able to conjointly negligible this state.
   GASES:-
Coming to the gases. These particles are not very closely packed as a result air particles move from area to area in a random direction if pressure and temperature are applied.

What will happen if particles move
There are 2 more conclusions I will discuss on this topic.

Conclusion 1:
When air conditioner and fan are used for the same time. The cooler particles are denser than hot air particles and then hot air moves upwards and cool air remains at the bottom.
The cooler particles from the air conditioner rotate around the atmosphere with help of fan air.

What changes may take place is
1. "When these particles rotate around the atmosphere every particle get collides with other particles as a result particles get heated up due to friction and move up due to their lightweight.
As we all know that air moves from high pressure to low pressure. As a result hot air moves upward there may be a chance of a decrease in air pressure in that area hence cold

air from surrounding areas moves towards the low-pressure area and balance the atmosphere

But if the movement of particles is incredibly high then there will be a rapid collision and hence hot air moves upwards within a no span.

Hence, we will find no modification in the temperature of that area."

Conclusion 2:-

Hot air moves up and cold is present in the bottom portion. The hot air particles are again cooled up by the air conditioning i.e air conditioner cools air particles that are present in and out of a room and hence there will be a slight difference in temperature in that area. There will also increase in the work of an air conditioning. If the work of air conditioning increases the rate of power consumption also increases.

Eventually, I would like to suggest using ac and fan at the same time will not disperse cold air but instant heating of that dispersion of cold air takes place if you want both at a time u need to shut down all the windows and doors without leaving any air.

This is the scientific reason behind this life hack.

""We should be surrounded with fresh oxygen, not with chloro fluorocarbon.""

CHAPTER FIVE

BANNERS

""Banners will not make you popular or successful only your hard work and perseverance make you popular."

This topic is totally a novel.
"Do you know how banners really damage our economic system besides earth?"

Introduction:

"India is the only country, where people are being treated with utmost love and care. but because of no limitations to their love and respect, they are facing barriers.

In this topic, I am not criticizing or degrading their love but creating awareness among the people in such a way how banners result in the damage to our money which can be a public fund or private, and also our Environment."

Topic introduction:

"Banners and hoardings are used for advertisement purposes, functions, commercials or to point out their gratitude and love towards great personalities like politicians, actors etc. These are also accustomed to conveying information to people who don't seem to be much privy to that place or store or personality."

Usually, banners are of different sizes based on their purposes a typical square banner is that the one which has a dimension of 4ft (1.22 m) X 4ft (1.22 m) and a horizontal banner is having a dimension of 7ft (2.13 m) X 2ft (0.61 m).

Based on their usage banners are categorized into two types

1. Outdoor and Indoor type banners.

2. E — banners in gadgets.

Let us briefly look at these types

Indoor and outdoor banners:

Indoor and outdoor banners are prevalent in many rural and urban areas. Banners are plastic-like substances usually made from polyvinyl chloride chemicals.

Properties of Poly Vinyl Chloride

1. High durable nature.

2. Available at a cheap cost.

3. Having a great Tensile strength.

"Can polyvinyl chloride be used for another purpose?"

Yes, we are able to use polyvinyl chloride in pipes, construction materials, switchboards and for electric purposes.

Now the question of how it impacts the environment and human health.

Polyvinyl chloride is not an eco-friendly substance it emits volatile gases which are dangerous to human and causes respiratory problems to adults mostly in children it damages ambient air quality and pollutes those places.

Practically banners are made with polyvinyl chloride as these reduce cost and durability as told before.

Practically how does it impact?

We can find many banners in our nascent area. To make this concept more interesting, I will make you clear with an example

Let us take a road which is of 4 km for every 10 m there is a streetlight pole, therefore, the number of street poles is 400.

Let us consider a famous celebrity is born on so date usually fans or the people who love them will definitely attach a banner or flux boards to show their love.

The total number of banners is 400.

Let us assume the cost of a banner is 200 on an average

The total cost of 400 banners is 400×200 =80,000/-

I have taken 4 km which is around 80,000/-

Did you know what is the length of roadways in a state X?

It is nearly 14,723 km.

Let us consider it as 10,000 km

Total number of poles 10,000×1000/10 =10,00,000/-

cost is 10,00,000×200=20,00,00,000/-

Not a small amount if it is an election this amount may varies to 100cr.

It also varies with the popularity of that celebrity

Imagine festivals, birthdays, invitations etc. I have given an example of X then what about the remaining states.

Simply it's not a little amount.

If the same amount is used for development programs like the construction of roads, dams, and bridges most of the areas in a state get developed.

Impact On Environment:

Most of the people did not know what to do with all these banners as a result

They go for burning or incineration because of this act toxic gases are being released into atmosphere leading heavy damage.

What Precautions must government take?

1. Government must allow eco-friendly banners. Y government allowed those banners which are made up of cotton.
2. They should be biodegradable.
3. Less impact on the environment and releases fewer toxic elements into the atmosphere.
4. Excess usage of banners should be prohibited.
5. Should create awareness among people.
6. Should stop burning.

"I think the human stomach is lined with HCL to digest food but the earth isn't lined with acids to decompose banners."

E-banners:

- In order to avoid excess usage of indoor and outdoor banners and to spread information much earlier from one area to another electronic banners are used.
- It affects very lesson environment.
- Information from this type can be transported from one developed country to other

Eventually, I would like to conclude showing respect and gratitude towards your favourite personality just by attaching banners and flex will not satisfy your hero just do welfare work on their birthday like planting a tree, blood donation, food and cloth for the needy, or any other donations.

"

"IF 6 FEET CAN DECIDE YOUR FATE, THERE WILL BE A DAY WHEN YOU WON'T FIND FOOD ON YOUR PLATE.""

CHAPTER SIX

PART-1 SAFETY AND SECURITY

"EVERYONE IS EQUAL BEFORE THE LAW BUT IN INDIA MOSTLY IN RURAL AREAS, EVERYONE IS EQUAL BEFORE THE ENVIRONMENT ONLY."

In this essay, I am going to discuss one of the prodigious social issues facing INDIA.

It's about raping, molesting, and harassing a woman publicly as well as in the home. I will share my idea to ebb these problems.

Introduction:-

Before sharing my idea with you I would like to provide you with a brief introduction regarding this topic.

"Even in ancient times girls were used as slaves, they were not given enough respect. They were discriminated against because of their gender. They were used as slaves in some kingdoms, not allowed to enter temples, not allowed to attend gramasabhas, not allowed to sit beside husbands, and not allowed to come outside, in fact, in some instances women from raja fort were also not allowed. They were not allowed to develop themselves; they were not allowed to participate in meetings, and they were not allowed to remarry. These were some issues faced by women all over the world."

But what made women be a part of this society
During the time of warfare men actively participated and women were accustomed to acting as head of the family, managed households, supervising business, governed internal security. All these made women not at all a slave, but she is strong enough to face all the problems and issues concerning her family and some for society.
However, even during this contemporary time even menstruation and after pregnancy girls are being sent out from the village this could not be a positive sign in development. Even these conditions are present in contemporary society. They were not allowed to enter the temple. They were treated as a toy in this society.

Problems faced by girls in this present society.

- Lack of education.
- Domestic violence.
- Abusement.
- Rape and molesting.
- female infanticide.
- Not giving enough rights.
- Slaves in some places.
- PTSD

Even the government is taking necessary steps to decrease these kinds of activities but the potency of their work is not up to the mark

Steps were taken by the government.

- Providing reservations.
- Fir against these activities.
- Awareness campaigns.
- Empowering women in all aspects.

My idea is to decrease rape cases in India

- People from LGBT (GAY, TRANSGENDER) who are interested in driving auto-rickshaws are given a chance to ride after 8 PM in those areas wherever there is a risk for girls.
- GPS should be provided to each and every vehicle on the night shift.
- Internships associated with sex education should be mandatory for all students.
- With the help of students need to create awareness on IPC sections related to women.
- Self-defense camps, and analytical ability sessions ought to be conducted in each and every space.
- Cabs like UUBER and Oola should encourage girls, and widows to drive during the evening time by giving enough training.
- Awareness camps ought to be provided to women to survive from demand.

Recently the government of ANDHRA PRADESH started Disha app to save a girl or woman from being molested, this should be enforced throughout INDIA.

""Women's safety is our responsibility, not woman's.""

CHAPTER SEVEN

PART-2 10 LAWS EVERY WOMEN NEED TO KNOW

There are concerning 10 laws or rights that women ought to know. But most people are not even aware of those laws. They are being implemented to provide safety and security for a woman in our country. I will discuss these briefly in chronological order.

1. THE MATERNITY BENEFIT ACT, 1861

"According to this act, a lady employee who had been operational in a corporation for a span of a minimum of 80 days during 12 months preceding the date of her delivery was granted to take maternity advantages."

> *"Believe me, a baby bump weighs more than any other thing on the Earth."*

2. THE SPECIAL MARRIAGES ACT, 1954

"As we all knew that India was a land with diverse religions and caste systems however, in most cases article 15 was violated. However, in women, it had been associated with the unlawful activity to marry another caste because of their community norms and customs. This special marriage act helps in inter-caste marriages."

"Do you think this is often honest?"
If you're forced to marry someone of the same caste and religion instead of a person whom you have loved having a good attitude and behaviour...whom would you prefer?
In such instances, this special marriage act helps u to marry a person whom you wish.

""Marriages are not made in heaven but they are made to construct the heaven.""

3. THE DOWRY PROHIBITION ACT, 1961

"Do you think dowry plays a crucial role in marriages?"
I don't think so because it is not affordable to arrange the amount that is being asked by the bride groom's family. In India, most people are not in a position to understand the bride's situation and go for marriage without a dowry.
I think this is impossible. According to this act receiving dowry or giving dowry could be a serious offence. In some instances' the bridegroom's family demands a huge amount of dowry and if the bride's family is not in a position to give, then, the girl is being thrashed, harassed and sometimes succumbs.

""DO not worry my child, besides dowry, we have granted the permission for your in-laws to harass you, molest you and even kill you.""

4. THE INDIAN DIVORCE ACT, 1969

"This act allows the dissolution of marriage, and deserts their relationship, allowing them to remain separate with their mutual consent. Family courts are present to hear all the cases. These divorce cases are mainly due to misunderstanding, illegal affairs, and external and internal egos. In rural areas, people from both families sit and resolve as per the conditions whereas in urban areas even though houses are closely built But the process of applying and getting partitioned is very smooth. you are not only applying for divorce but also applying to damage children's life. Alimony is always a secondary thought."

""Divorce is common in other countries but in India, the damage is equally distributed among children and parents.""

5. THE MEDICAL TERMINATION OF PREGNANCY ACT, 1971.

"Nothing but an aborting. We were living in a society where a girl child was terminated within the womb of a woman. These cases had been flourishing for the last few decades although the government was taking necessary actions."
"Do you know a mother had a right to be defensive from terminating a child?"

The main aim of this act is to ebb or diminish all activities associated with terminating, mortality or morbidity.

""For most people, pregnancy is a boon. Don't terminate and dismantle the hope of a mother and toddler.""

6. THE EQUAL REMUNERATION ACT, 1976

"Women were discriminated against not solely in society but conjointly in payment. They were not given equal wages, salaries, or remuneration for their work in most of the MNC and other companies. The equal remuneration act helps in getting a fair price in any company or an organization. co-operation world transfer of money takes place from one hand to another. At the same time, the process of gaining money or giving money is not an easy task whereas in the corporate sector it is a bit difficult. That is why even though women's palms are smooth with no friction the money transfering or movement is very very tough. In these cases, men would not compete with women."

""Equal remuneration is nothing but Equal importance. We call a particular thing an important only if we know the value of that thing.""

7. THE INDECENT REPRESENTATION OF WOMEN (PREVENTION) ACT, 1986

"These acts prohibit indecent writings on women in public places, and in paintings. We can see those in many public areas and toilets. If you guys really think indecent painting gives much happiness then draw those painting which depicts the pain when a woman is giving birth, and pain during period cramps."

""Drawing indecent pictures about a woman does not mean you are a winner. Drawing others' attention just by speaking about women is an ultimate victory.""

8. THE NATIONAL COMMISSION FOR WOMEN ACT, 1990.

It was a statutory body that came into existence in Jan 1992. It provides a stand on issues and concerns associated with women.

The main objective is to increase the status of women and empowerment.

> *""Women empowerment means giving freedom and importance in every aspect and considering her opinion."*
> *"*

9. THE PROHIBITION OF CHILD MARRIAGE ACT, 2006

"Child marriages are one of the evil customs in our society a girl was forced to marry at a young age. This has been adopted from the past centuries because these girls were not even getting a basic education in our society. This act was fortified in 2007 according to this act the marriages which subjected under 18 girls and 21 boys were illegal. They shall have a right to go for legal aid. Most of the children get benefited because of this act.

> *""Child marriages are like fungus. We know that fungus cause is due to moist conditions just like that child marriages are happening in rural areas due to lack of education."*
> *"*

10. THE SEXUAL HARASSMENT OF WOMEN AT WORKPLACES ACT, 2013

A girl was sexually harassed all her way from house to work in some organizations' girl was sexually harassed in the office by using abusive language, molesting and touching. This act helps a girl to fight these situations in office and alternate personal corporations.f

> *"Sexual harassment declines faith and belief. These can be eradicated just by eradicating those thoughts."*

There are also some rights that the women need to know

- If a girl or lady was accused of a crime she should be interrogated only by a female constable.
- She should not be allowed to stay in PS after 6 PM.
- She should be produced in a court within 24 hrs.
- A woman should not be taken into custody after 6 PM.
- There are also other instances like ZERO First Information Report.
- According to this a girl can register FIR in PS which is nearer to her and this FIR is being transported to the respective area police station.
- FIR can be of email, video or written.

But most people did not know about these things.
I aim to create awareness among girls concerned about these acts and rights.

> *"Customs what we are following, just the cover page of a book. Education and knowledge are what we need to earn."*

CHAPTER EIGHT

LGBT

Hello all!!!!!!!!!!!!
Let's start with questions.

1. "Have you ever heard about LGBT?"
2. "Did you find any transgender in INDIAN ARMY or NAVY?"If not why?
3. "Is it not an article 15 violation?"
4. "Why they are prejudiced in this society?"
5. "Aren't they humans?"
6. "Because of the hormonal changes they are treated as 3rd category....Is this their fault?"
7. "Then why they were being differentiated by the people in this society?"
8. "Do you apprehend what rights have been incurred by SC?"

This article is not for the sake of my learning we have to treat people equally nevertheless their caste, sex, creed, or religion.

It is very important for us to make them realize and to educate them about what necessary rights the supreme court had given for their all-round development

Before aiming to start this article, I would like to give a

piece of small information regarding article 15

What article 15 says is no one is discriminated against because of caste, Creed, sex, religion or any other basis.

As our country is diversified with different relations, caste systems, and creeds but why do the people show partiality concerning gender....

Introduction

While travelling on the roads, train or any other means of transport system we tend to come across many transgenders, and we were forced to give money.

We always criticize them for their way of dressing, attitude and other aspects. But deep inside they are also humans who are seeking love, caring as well as respect in our society,

They are about 5,00,000 transgenders in our country the number has been rapidly increasing over the last couple of years.

History

- Transgenders were present not only in this contemporary society but also present in the epic Mahabharat. Have you come across a name shikhandi, brother of Draupadi who was a transgender in Mahabharata? He completely changed the result of the Kurukshetra war. Initially, he was a female and later transformed into male
- Transgender people are accustomed to worshipping Bahuchar Mata who was treated as a goddess of fertility.
- Many scriptures had drawn the nature of the transgenders. The main scriptures called Sushruta Samhita and Charaka Samhita are concerned with the

issues of homosexuality. Homosexuality was mainly due to the scanty sperm of the male.

- There are many punishments if the people in the ancient time get caught in this kind of activities
- According to Manu Smriti, the punishments like imposing a fine of 200 coins, 100 whiplashes, a head shaved off and two fingers were cut and was made them ride on a donkey. Punishment is like loss of caste in the case of men.
- Because of the swift evolution of civilization in the pre-colonial period, the people did not criminalize these activities.
- Whereas in the British period article 377 was completely prohibited and was made an offence. Severe punishments were imposed if they were caught doing these activities.
- Even after independence prohibition practice has been continued. With the proliferating nature of our society, this culture had also been enriching but legal permission was not given.
- In the year 2009, there was a court case between the Naz Foundation and the government of Delhi regarding the prohibition against this was the fundamental right violation as it violates the Right to life or privacy, it was also violating articles 15 and 19.
- They would be punished for this offence with life or 10 years.
- On 28 February 2012 Ministry of Human affairs Expressed its opposition to homosexual activity stating it as Immoral activity again in March the minister of human affairs changed the change decision stating that it was violating the fundamental right.

- In December 2015 Shashi Tharoor introduced this law to repeal Section 377 but it was rejected by the house on basis of a vote.
- Again in 2016 SC decided to review the criminalization of human sex activity
- After lots of hearing in August 2017, Supreme Court declared the right to individual privacy is an intrinsic and fundamental right. This indirectly gave hope to many transgenders.
- On 6 September 2018 judgement was password legalizing human sexuality in India.

So, the next thing is we have to find what per cent are present in this category

There was a survey conducted on behalf of the Government of India on this topic. I would like to share with you an updated detail

A survey was conducted by Ipsos (LGBT plus Pride India 2021 Global survey) between April and May 2021.

The report consists of the following survey details.

- About 2% of the Indian population has not yet decided whether they are male or female(transgender)
- About 3% of our country is homosexual (attracted to the same gender)
- 9% bisex(both genders)
- 1% Pan sex (regardless of Gender and identity)
- 2% Asexual.

State laws and rights

To flourish their life and increase their standard of living governments of different states have taken this as a challenge and started implementing many laws and schemes.

1. The first and the foremost transgender policy was introduced by the states of Tamil Nadu and Kerala. In that policy states had implemented free sex reassignment surgery, provided free housing, admissions to the government college and various welfare schemes.
2. West Bengal set up a transgender welfare community board in the year 2015.
3. Himachal Pradesh had started medical boards a district and state levels for assisting transgender pensions scholarships and medical assignments.
4. In the year 2017 Ministry of drinking and sanitation instructed all states to Allow transgenders or any other from the LGBT category to use public toilets of their own choice.
5. Chandigarh and Karnataka have started social welfare programs and health professional programmes.
6. Coming to Andhra Pradesh in the year 2017, Pension plans had been introduced by CBN as a part of it 1500 per month was sanctioned to the transgenders, provided ration cards, house sites, scholarship for education, subsidy bus pass and granted loans. It was repealed by YS Jaganmohan Reddy and enlarged pension up to 3000

Although they were given many schemes, and welfare programs their position in society had not been changing but most of the people showed partiality.

This was one of the Evil problems that have been facing by them.

They were not allowed to sit beside us in some places,

they were not allowed to enter society, people feel that they had become a nuisance, they were not called for any other interviews or in other sectors for doing a job, and they were not given enough respect and identity but what happening was they were completely vexed with the nature of the biased society and as a result of this opted to create a nuisance.

Earlier they were discriminated against for studying in schools and colleges and discriminated against from doing any job but after judgement, in the year 2018-2019 many rules and rights got enforced, and they were entitled to many laws and rights.

If govt concerned about transgender then why did not we find any transgender in the military?

In the year 2018, a bill was introduced regarding transgender services in the military but it lapsed in Lok Sabha that may be so many reasons. After that, the bill has not been reintroduced.

THEIR HEALTH CONDITION WILL NOT SUPPORT THEM TO GAIN FITNESS. I hope they will get a chance to work in the MTS sector in military services.

What rights did the transgender possess?

- Family- no child shall be separated from the parents based on being transgender without The Contempt of court
- They have the right to live in households and to enjoy facilities that are present in the house. They were not prohibited from exploiting any household equipment

- Education- transgender should not be discriminated against or neglected or harassed because of sex in schools and colleges. They should be given enough freedom to learn with a peer group.
- No people shall discriminate against transgender like
- Unfair treatment in Educational Institutes.
- Unfair treatment in employment
- Unfair treatment in Health Care Centers
- Unfair treatment to access any goods and services and accommodate in any area auto utilize any facilities that are being utilized by a common people
- Not permitting right of movement
- Not allowing residing, purchase, rent
- Not allowing starting new institutions, holding public or private organizations.
- Parents who are unable to take care of court shall return the order and direct the person to be placed in the rehabilitation centre.
- There are also many offences most the people were not much aware of
- If They were not allowed to work
- If there are blockaded from using public places
- Arms and injuries were mentally or physically is a serious offence

For all the above statements the punishment would be up to 6 months about 2 years in some cases and also fines.

Although they are many schemes and acts that are completely supporting the life of transgender there are beneath levels in this contemporary society

Orissa started SWEEKRUTI to ensure opportunities, and employment and to create facilities.

if you feel like respecting them is awkward and then don't

criticize them for your awkwardness………

Jai hind...

Most of the data present here is extracted and modified from google and books read by me. well, my only aim is to reach the importance of transgender and their rights to many people.

CHAPTER NINE

PREGNANT LADY

""A BABY BUMP HAS AN ABILITY TO CREATE ALL EMOTIONS AT THE SAME TIME""

when I was asked to deliver a seminar on any of the topics, I had been through this pregnancy topic. Being an engineering student and male, did u want to know how I managed this topic.

This subject is extremely complicated to understand. But as a human, it is our responsibility to grasp the issues that a pregnant woman faces.

But before visiting this subject let me ask you a question.

"We, humans, have the same number of bones, body parts, same organs but my question is how an archaeological department finds whether this body belongs to a male or female if it doesn't have any ornaments or attires?"

Due to an incredible increase in science and technology, the carbon dating method is being employed but when 50 years or 100 years ago there is no sufficient technology to search out whose body or skeleton it is.

But ancient scriptures mentioned the difference between

men and women that is the pelvic bone which presents just below the abdomen.

Yes, in males this part is narrower compared to females.

"But why?"

Because in pregnancy stage female body requires another space to make her baby grow. how beautiful the god's creation, that is why the female pelvic portion is much wider than the male.

This topic is completely for men to grasp what care has to be taken when your wife, your sister, or other is pregnant.

Impacts due to pregnancy :

- Not able to face it for hours.
- Vomiting at regular time intervals as a result of energy loss is more.
- Sometimes dizziness and the body becomes really weak.
- Fingers become swollen and make it difficult to steer or try any work.
- Sometimes labour pains make it difficult to move.
- The overall change in their body.

What should we suppose to do are:

- We should share their household chores like cleaning, washing and sometimes cooking.
- Love and caring are very important. The only person she is seeking for hard things is you so never disrespect her, or degrade her.
- Make her feel comfortable, just give her strength just by standing beside her.
- Sometimes massaging her feet or legs.

- Giving her medicines regularly.
- Don't show any rude, reckless behaviour to her.
- Cook her something special and surprise her but please don't do any experiments.
- Spend some time with her and humorously talk with her.

What pregnant women are supposed to do

- She should take a good and healthy diet.
- Following the doctor's instructions carefully.
- Don't attempt to do complicate work like holding heavy objects or bending heavily.
- Regular small exercise or yoga should be done.
- Should not move out during eclipse time powerful UV rays may impact inside baby.
- Don't suppose to clean cat waste as cat waste contains highly toxic elements which can affect you.
- Water should be taken at regular time intervals.

Eventually, why I have chosen the topic is, that we will see many pregnant ladies standing on buses and metro railways because of no seat to sit, maybe we can't share her pain, but we can give them our seats.

Respect them because they are responsible for our generation's growth.

In some countries like Japan and other developed, pregnant woman was given a card. She can sit in any position where she wanted to. why can't our country or state provide facilities like those to them?

What steps should government must dream for pregnant

ladies

1. Providing special seats to them in trains and buses.

2. Giving them priority in the medicinal aspect

3. Illegal sex-determining scanning centres should be noticed and necessary actions should be taken.

"A woman's happiness depends on her husband's care and baby's growth."

CHAPTER TEN

FARMERS

***"FARMERS ARE THE FRAMERS OF OUR
SOCIETY. RESPECT AND HONOUR THEM."***

<u>ABOUT FARMERS</u>

India is my country all Indians are my brothers and sisters; I love my country .... These are the things that we have come across in our school days but do you know our brothers and sisters who are working in the agriculture sector are not even getting what they want. In this article, we want to share a few things about farmers in India.

A few decades earlier the population of India is not greater than 1 million. The food products that are produced during that time is sufficient for them, and they are healthy and organic. But the population explosion took place in the 19th and 20th century hence the food products required is more to meet the needs of every human as a result usage of pesticides and chemicals came into existence. But nearly 90% of Indian farmers are not well-educated they did not know how to use pesticides or any other chemicals as the result the production is quite low than expected. Another thing that damages their work is the market rate. Their product did not get a minimum market rate. Due to unfair conditions, debt with a lot of interest etc. leads them to take a decision not even a single person wants that is suicide. To reduce these things govt. started many schemes like low-interest debt, free pesticides and manure distribution but all these do not even decrease the death rate of farmers. Some statistics:

· India is the 1st largest producer of cotton, with an average of 60 farmers committing suicide every day.

· West Bengal is the largest producer of rice; Maharashtra is the 1st state more than 4000 farmers commit suicide as per 2012 statistics more than 23,000 farmers have committed suicide in the state of Maharashtra from 2009-to 16.

· National report by NCRB, the state with the highest incidence of farmer suicide in 2015 were Maharashtra (3030), Telangana (1358), and Andhra Pradesh (739).

Why they are committing suicide:

- Lack of irrigation.
- Unsuitability of seeds.
- Inadequate source of credit.
- Debts.
- Pests and other problems.

Solution: To provide minimum solutions to decrease suicides we the students formed a group. The aim of us is to create awareness among the farmers as well as in society. so we went village by village and motivated many farmers and gave our ideas. They were too impressed by our ideas. Some of them are

· Card system in agriculture.

· Land shifting process in agriculture.

· Water management in Agriculture .etc.

Conclusion: Farmers are the backbone of our country. When someone asks you who is your grandfather you will answer that he is a farmer but when the same question is asked to your grandchild, he will answer engineer or doctor but not a farmer. So plz respect and protect our Kohinoor diamonds...

" *We, the farmers looking for arms, not for alms*"

CHAPTER ELEVEN

ORPHANAGE

" "Once organizations are used to run for those children who died in the war but now f0r those who were fed up with their children."

ORPHANAGES

Introduction:- India is a land with different people, different organizations, customs and traditions. Besides these orphanages, old age homes etc. are also prevalent in India. During the traditional times, most of the people called Indian people to favour more relations which may be friends, family and others. But in this contemporary society, these family relations are getting fade away as a result orphanages and old age homes number gradually increasing.

In this topic, we Shall be discussing orphanages, not in India but also in different areas and countries.

History of an Orphanage :

The word orphanage is not a new word it is familiar to all ancient people. Romans were the primary ones to make the orphanage system in this world according to them orphanage may be a place or home where children are present whose parents are succumbed, widows, or old ages people care for. In the olden days, there are many wars as the result most of their parents get fatalities. As a result, there is none to seem after the children. So, at that time orphanages are formed not only Romans, Jews, Iran's and many kings of that time supported these orphanages.

There are also many Synonyms for orphanages like foundling child, Asylum care, Orphan hood etc.

Orphanages in India :

In the olden days there are many joint families in every family there could also be nearly 10-15 members .unfortunately if someone in that family had deceased there were others to look after. In this contemporary society due to less number of individuals in houses orphanages houses getting increased.

In one of the journals, the ad has mentioned that 4 out of 5 members in an orphanage house had one among their parents but what made their hitch in the orphanage was their poverty. Taking this as an advantage most people sell their babies or use them as beggars and increase their business. Although the government is taking many precautions and necessary to drop off the chance of selling and buying is not at all changing.

<u>**How to start an orphanage :**</u>

Most people want to do social service. They always starve to serve their country by establishing Orphanage homes and Old age homes.

Below are the main important steps to start an orphanage

- Decide your location where you would like to start an organization.
- Register your orphanage home and the er FOREIGN REGULATION AND CONTRIBUTION ACT.
- Create a bank account for donations.
- Certificate of 80G should be taken to exempt from taxes from charter accountants.
- Should submit what reasonably provisions that you are going to live in like food, sanitation, education etc.
- Should have a skilled person who always rummages around for organization and child improvement.
- Should advertise yourself about this funding organization.
- Most important thing is your dedication and service nature.

Then why it is difficult to get permission from the government :
we are looking at only one side of a coin but the other side is very scary

- Child sex abuse cases increasing
- Funds and donations are not used in an appropriate manner.
- The development of the child is not good.
- Some of the fake organizations are forming and selling babies or children for prime costs to the organizations and even use them as sex workers.
- Education and development are neglected in most orphanages.

"How children are being affected?"

- Not getting enough love from parents
- Mental suffering
- Always criticizing their fate
- Some are committing suicide.
- Overall development is incredibly less than a result they are turning into evils in our society

"Can we minimize Orphanages in our country ??"
Yes, we can just by adopting them. India is not a small country or poor country it has sufficient funds, and and and and human resources and many are interested in adopting an an an an anana an a children.
Believe it or not when I was a child I thought of adopting a toddler after getting 22 years no matter about marriage. Legally it is impossible to adopt a child but my idea always makes me proud. Why can't you guys who are married adopt a child?
If you can donate money to someone then why can't you donate your love and time just by adopting them?
The only thing that one can give to another with no cost is. love and caring.
Thank you for your support and love.

"Earlier, there is a statement like OLD IS GOLD but now, it is rearranged as OLD CAN BE SOLD."

CHAPTER TWELVE

FLOODS

""Water has the property to take a shape of any container, believe me it hasn't excluded humans."

INTRODUCTION: -

We may have seen lots of floods in our life, but we did not know how in-depth floods affect humans, animals, aquatic life, agriculture, and industries. It also causes huge damage to valuable properties. In this lesson, you will come across how floods are formed, types of floods, how floods are useful in some cases, how floods affect humans, animals and also damage to property taking Kerala floods which were occurred in mid-august 2018.

DEFINITION:

Floods may be defined as the swift movement of water having high discharge that sinks terrestrial areas partially or fully. Flooding may occur as an overflow of water from rivers, lakes, or oceans in which water overtops or breaks levees. Resulting in the escape of water from its boundaries. Usually, levees are the weakest portion to get damaged easily. Hence, in case of overflow usually, water tries to escape from the fixed path and applies pressure along the channel. If the discharge of water is very high it breaks the weakest portion and flows out. One of the deadliest floods occurred in China effected nearly 25millions in 1931.

TYPES OF FLOODS:
Floods may be classified on the basics of the duration, come and damage. These may be classified into 3 types

- Flash floods.
- Rapid on set floods.
- Slow on set floods.

Let us discuss the types of floods.

Flash Floods: -

- Flood that occurs in a very short span.
- Occur without any prediction.
- These floods are mainly caused due to heavy rain, sudden dam break or due to melting of snow on mountains due to global warming.
- It lasts for 2-4 hours.
- Vandalizing property is high
- 1924 Kerala floods come under this category.
- No warning, no preparation and impact are swift and devasting.

Rapid on set floods: -

- Flood takes a longer duration to develop.
- It lasts for a two to three days based on its intensity

- These floods are very destructive but not quick as flash floods.
- Although flood is very destructive if necessary steps are taken people can survive easily.

Slow on set floods:-

- 1. Slow on set floods may be defined as the floods which are very slow to develop compared to flash floods and rapid on set floods
- 2. Lasts for days or weeks.
- 3. These floods spread over kilometres and occur more in flood plains.
- 4. People can easily escape if measures are taken but the only problem is due to the floods snakes easily enter houses causing deaths due to snake bites
- 5. Malnutrition will also take place.

Causes of floods: -

floods are mainly caused due to following reasons

- Too many rains cause water to flow overland rivers or streams can overflow through their banks.
- Streams hold more water upstream than usual flow down streams sudden discharge may lead to flooding
- Dam is used to hold water flowing down, electricity is generated through potential energy stored in a dam. when sudden breakage of the dam leads to flooding.
- If the temperature increases due to global warming results in the melting of glaciers and finally leads to flooding. Due to the slope of mountains water flows

with great speed leads to flooding or discharge is more.
- Rainfall-runoff can't be channelled appropriately into the drainage system forcing the water to flow overland. Land of drainage leads to flooding
- If there is no vegetation there is a little stoppage of rainwater from running off leads to floods.
- Damage to power transmission: it also impacts power transmission and interrupts the power flow.

Secondary effects: -

- Decline in tourism.
- Rebuilding cost.
- loss of property.
- Respiratory effect.

Benefit causes due to floods: -

- Recharging groundwater.
- Increasing nutrients in the soil.
- Helpful in an arid and semi-arid climate.
- Improves pisciculture.
- Kills pests.
- Ancient monuments or other materials can be transported or uplifted.

Methods to control floods: -

- Retaining walls: - To prevent flood flow during an emergency.
- Town planning: - Proper drainage system should be provided such that rainwater flows very quickly so there

will be no stagnation.

- Vegetation: - If the forest area is more there will be a slow movement of rainwater resulting in a decrease in floods.
- Educate people: - Educate people and make them aware of how floods affect and also preventive measures to be taken during floods.

Planning for floods safety: -

- Observation of previous and present flood heights.
- Mapping flood scenario.
- Engineering designs and construction of the structure to control flood..
- Monitoring regularly.
- Long term land use and regulations.

> *"Two things need to remember when dealing with the sea.*
>
> *It's hard to determine Its length when we go over the sea and its weight when it comes upon us."*

Conclusion: - Floods are mainly caused due to deforestation, mining, construction etc. To control floods, we have to take necessary measurements or else we have to be ready to fight for our lives.

> *"Flood changes the length of human life measures modern machines, challenges the human brain, sweeps its slot and revolts for its territory."*

CHAPTER THIRTEEN

KERALA ELEPHANT

One of the most heartbreaking incidents that have ever occurred in Kerala desecrated human nature.

"Was it an unlucky occurrence or was it a dreadful incident?"

Let's take a look at what's transpired.

Two innocent creatures got killed in June as a result of an act by tribals and farmers.

It occurred in the peaceful valley of Kerala's Palakkad district, which is recognised as God's creation.

"However, what had occurred?"

Boars in that area used to destroy all food crops, causing massive crop damage and destroying and destroying many farmers' livelihoods. Farmers chose to use fireworks to kill boars to safeguard vegetation and food crops. They set off pyrotechnics in a pineapple to catch and entrap them.

Unfortunately, that pineapple was eaten by a 14-year-old elephant with a baby in its stomach. The crackers in her stomach began to rupture in a short period, and the young elephant died as a result.

The mother elephant, on the other hand, felt a scorching feeling in her tummy. To relieve the discomfort, it went to a nearby river and drank water, staying in the river for nearly two days. The elephant's mouth broke into bits, rendering him unable to eat or drink. Due to a lack of food and burn illnesses, the elephant died two days after the incident. This act shattered people's faith in mankind.

Even though the people in that region did not want to murder elephants, two elephants died as a result of their activities.

They had been set on fire by the people. This experience shifted not just human perceptions of humans, but also animal perceptions of humans.

So, can farmers or tribals have a legal right to kill animals?

They do not have the authority to kill. There are a variety of additional methods for putting a halt to boars, such as Sound speakers, black crows, and sound crackers.

Boars can also be caught using traps. However, killing is said to be a sin.

The same thing happened to a cow in Andhra Pradesh. Two days later, her mouth was destroyed.

> *""IF YOU WANT TO CATCH A BOAR, YOU HAVE TO START THINKING LIKE A BOAR NOT LIKE A HUMAN.""*

BIOLOGY

A flower is something which brings green culture, fragrance, and ornamental purpose and gives a pleasant odour. In this, I am going to share a few things related to flowers and their features.

#POST-1#

- Study of flowers is called FLORICULTURE.
- Telugu name:- Roja Puvvu.
- Latin(botanical) name of Rose:- Rosa.
- Scientific name of pink rose:- Rose bridal pink.
- There are about a hundred different species of Roses.

Enter Caption

- Soil conditions:- Loamy soil.
- Roses are the symbol of love and affection.
- Pandit Jawaharlal Nehru used to pin a rose to his pocket which resembles affection and love for our country and children.
- Colour resemblance and its symbols.

- Pink:- Admiration, joy, gratitude and love.
- Light pink:- Pleasantness and innocence.
- Dark pink:- Gratitude and appreciation.

#POST- 2#

- Study of flowers is called FLORICULTURE.
- Kanakambaram isae word derived from Malayalam.

FIRECRACKER

- THE GOLDEN BEAUTY OF THE GARDEN.
- English name:- firecracker flower.

- Meaning of this flower's colour and beauty.
- Scientific name:- Crossandra infundibulumformis.
- Family:- Acanthaceae.
- Soil conditions:- Peat soil.
- Plant uses:- Antibacterial, Aphrodisiac, Bronchitis, Cough, Liver problems, Menstrual Disorders, Cold, Cough, Wounds.

#POST -3#

- Study of the flower is called FLORICULTURE.
- Telugu name:- Banthi Puvvu.
- English name :- Marigold or Tagetes.

Mari gold

- Scientific name:- Tagetes Erecta.
- Family:- Daisy's family.
- Common name or another name:- Pot marigold, Poets marigold, Scott's marigold.
- Uses:- Medicine:- Injurious inflammation, wound healing for sunburns.

#POST- 4#

- Study of the flower is called FLORICULTURE.
- Telugu name :- Thangedu.
- English (botanical)name:- Senna Auriculate(cassia auriculate).
- Subfamily:- Caesalpinioideae.
-

Senna Auriculate

- Common name:- Avaram, Matura tea.
- Speciality:- State flower of Telangana.
- Uses:- Roots are used in precautions against fever, diabetes and disease of urinary,
- mainly used as sacred flowers at the Bathukamma festival.

#POST - 5#

- Study of flowers is called FLORICULTURE.
- Telugu name:- Roja Puvvu.
- Latin(botanical) name of Rose:- Rosa.
- Scientific name of white ose - Rosa × alba.
- There are about a hundred different species of Roses.
- Soil conditions:- Loamy soil.
- Rose colour and its symbols.
- Pink:- Admiration, joy, gratitude and love.
- Light pink:- pleasantness and innocence.
- Dark pink:- gratitude and appreciation.

Rosa

#POST- 6#

- Study of birds is called ORNITHOLOGY.
- Chicken - an immature or at least young Bird.
- Telugu name:- Kodi for female, Punju for male.
- English name = Rooster/Cock (male name).

- Hen For the female name.
- Younger male = Cockerel.
- Immature female= Bullet.
- Lifespan = 5 to 10 years.
- belongs to 2 omnivores.
- Scientific name = Gal Gal domestic service.
- Biddy = a newly hatched chicken.

Rooster/Cock (male name)

<u>**#POST-7#**</u>

- Study of the flower is called FLORICULTURE.
- Telugu name:- jilledu(killed).
- English name:- CALATROPIS GIGANTIC.
- Family:- APOCYNACEAE.
- Binomial name:- Calotropis gigantia.
- Contains five-pointed Petals.
- Uses:- Digestive disorders including diarrhoea, stomach ulcers, toottoothachesamps and joint pains.
- Common name:- milkweeds.
- poisonous plants.
- Harmful to the eyes.
- Offered to Hindu deities Shiva and Ganesh.

CALATROPIS GIGANTIC

- Telugu name:- Seethamma vaari jada plant..
- English name:- Cockscomb
- Family:- Amaranth family, AmaranthaceaeDerived from the Greek word meaning "Burning."
- Common name:- Woolflowers, Celosia, Pattu Tulsa flower, Jyada Bianchi.
- Uses:- As a garden plant, food, Mostly used in Bathukamma festival, Medicine to treat skin problems.
- In Mexico it is known as the VELVET flower.

Cockscomb

- NIGERIA is known as SOKOYOKOTO meaning "husbands fat and happy."
- In SPAIN known as ROOSTER COMB because of its presence.
- Soil conditions/ Environmental conditions:- Humid areas, don't need moderate soil moisture.

<u>**#POST-9#**</u>

- Study of the flower is called FLORICULTURE.
- Telugu name:- Banthi Puvvu.
- English name :- Marigold or Tagetes.

Marigold

- Scientific name:- Tagetes Erecta.
- Family:- Daisy's family.

- Common name or another name:- Pot marigold, Poets marigold, Scott's marigold.
- Uses:- Medicine:- Injurious inflammation, wound healing for sunburns.

#POST- 10#

- • Study of Gastropods(Greek means stomach foot) is called Conchology(study of mollusc shells) means "creeping thing."
- conchologists mainly deal with
  - gastropods (snails)
  - bivalves (clams)
  - Polyplacophora(chitons)
  - Scaphopoda(tusk shells)
- Protects from predators, damage, dehydration, muscle flexibility and Calcium storage.
- Three major layers
- calcareous central layer- trace -mare made of calcium carbonate.

Gastropods

- outermost layer -periostracum - resistant to abrasion.
- inner layer conchiolin on periostracum.
- most shells are spirally coiled.

- if the shell becomes significantly broken then the snail will die as the shell provides protection.
- snail life - 2-3 years.
- snails have very bad eyesight and won't recognhumansuman.
- uses:- ceramics, paint, animal feed, construction and paper industry. Commonly used as fish bait.

#POST- 11#

- Study of arthropods is called Arthropodology.....
- English name:- Millipede.
- Telugu name:- Bahupaadi.
- Kingdom:- Animalia.
- Phylum:- Arthropoda.
- Most millipedes are slow-moving detritivores, eating decaying leaves and other dead plant matter.
- These are generally not harmful to you.
- Excess rain, drought and cooler temperature make them live outside.
- Unlike centipedes these are non-poisonous.

Millipede

- Study of the flower is called FLORICULTURE.
- Telugu name:- Banthi Puvvu.
- English name :- Marigold or Tagetes.

Marigold or Tagetes

- Scientific name:- Tagetes Erecta.
- Family - Daisy's family.
- Common name or another name:- Pot marigold, Poets marigoldScott'sts marigold.
- Uses:- Medicine:- Injurious inflammation, wound healing for sunburns.

#POST- 13#

- Telugu name:- (gaddi puvvu).
- English name:- Moss rose.
- Scientific name:- Portulacaceae.

Moss rose

- Family:- Purslane.
- It is used in the treatment of hepatitis, cirrhosis of the liver with ascites, swelling and pain in the pharynx.
- Soil conditions:- dry soil and warm condition..

#POST-14#

- Telugu name:- Talambralu Chettu.
- English name:- Lantana camara.
- family:- Verbenaceae.

Lantana camara

- genus:- Lantana. Other common names of L. Camara:- big-sage (Malaysia), wild-sage, red-sage, white-sage (Caribbean), kors wire or korsoe wire (Suriname), tick Berry (South Africa),
- West Indian lantana, umbelanterna, putus in Bengal and Gu Phool in Assam, India.
- It is a perennial plant and is toxic to livestock to graze.

- uses:- Lantana leaves can Show antimicrobial, fungicidal and insecticidal properties.
- o L.camara has also been used in traditional herbal medicines for treating a variety of ailments, including cancer, skin itches, leprosy, chicken pox, measles, asthma and ulcers.

<u>#POST- 15#</u>

- Study of flowers is called floriculture.
- Telugu Name:- Bogada banthi puvvu.
- English name:- vadamalli, Gomphrena globosa, Makhmali, globe amaranth.
- Family:- Amaranthaceae.

Vadamalli

- Kingdom:- Plantae
- Mythology:- These are liked a much by the godshiva and kumaraswamy.
- These are perennial plants.
- Chemicals that are present.
- Flavonoids.
- Betacyanins.
- Volatiles.

- Uses:-

- o In Nepal these are known as Makhmali these are used to make garlands and these garlands are put around brothers' necks by their sisters for protection.
- o Herbal medicines.
- o Used for baby Gripe, cough and diabetes, several respiratory inflammations including asthma, acute and chronic bronchitis, whooping cough, respiratory diseases, jaundice, urinary system and kidney problems.
- o Used in the food industry, cosmetics and livestock.

o Growth conditions:- heat tolerant and fairly drought resistant.

#POST -16#

- Study of flowers is called Floriculture.
- Telugu name:- Malle puvvu (chukka malle)
- English name:- Jasmine.
- Taxonomic name:- Jasminum.
- Family:- Oleaceae.

- Kingdom:- Plantae.
- Jasminum Fluminense (which is sometimes known by the inaccurate name "Brazilian Jasmine"), Jasminum dichotomum (Gold Coast Jasmine), Jasminum Polyanthum also known as White Jasmine

- Uses:-

- Fragrance.
- Jasmine tea in china.
- Plantation.
- Decorative purpose.

- National flower

- Several countries and states consider jasmine a National symbol.
- It's a national flower of Syria, Pakistan, Philippines, Indonesia etc
- City of jasmine:- Damascus

- Growth conditions:- Tropical and Warm temperate regions.

Jasmine.

#POST- 17#

- Telugu name:- Gaddi puvvu.
- English name:- Moss rose.
- Family:- Purslane.
- It is used in the treatment of hepatitis, Cirrhosis of the liver with ascites, swelling and pain in the pharynx.
- Soil conditions:- Dry soil highlight and warm condition...
- It becomes neutralised in the Mediterranean region.
- Scientific name:- Portulacaceae.

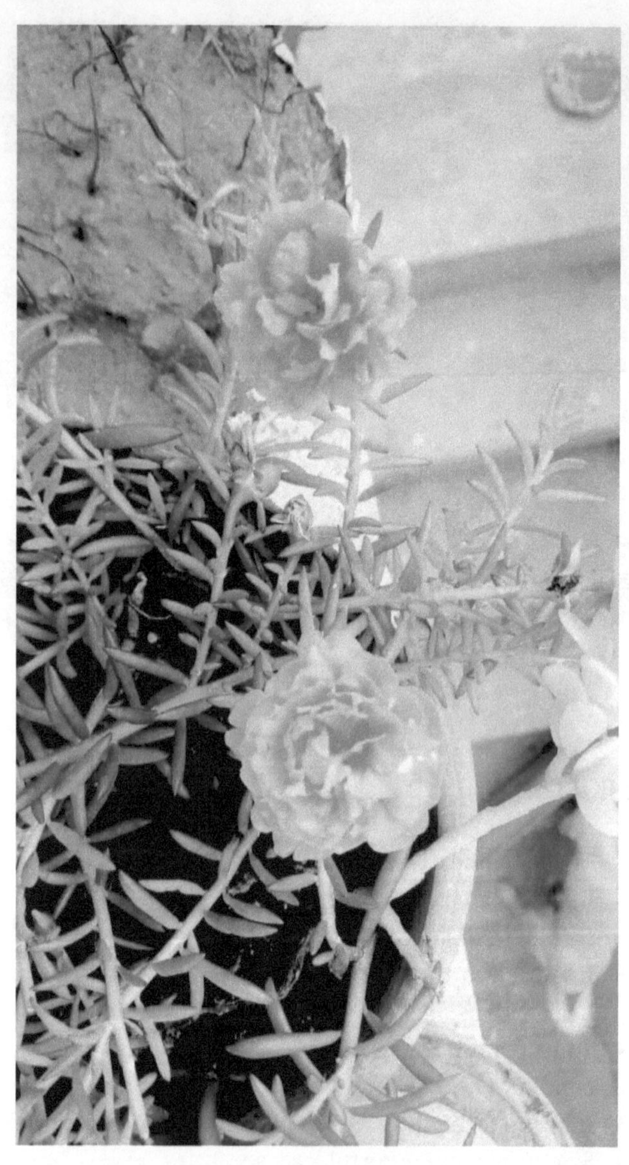

Moss rose

#POST- 18#

- Study of flowers is called Floriculture.
- Telugu name:- Mandaaram.
- English name:- Hibiscus rosa-Sinensis.
- Taxonomic name:- Hibiscus Rosa-Sinensis.
- Family:- Malvaceae.
- Kingdom:- Plantae.

Uses:-

- Hair care.
- Shine shoes.
- ph indicator(When used, the flower turns acidic solutions to a dark pink or magenta colour and basic solutions to green).
- Worship.
- Used in Beverages, usually tea.
- Ornamental plant.
- Plantation.
- Decorative purpose.
- National flower.
- Several countries and states consider this a National symbol.

It's a national flower in Malaysia and an unofficial national flower in Haiti.

Growth conditions:- Tropical and Subtropical regions.

Hibiscus rosa-Sinensis

<u>#POST-19#</u>

- Telugu name:- Talambralu Chettu.
- English name:- Lantana camara.
- Family:- Verbenaceae.

Lantana camara

- Other common names of L. Camara:- Big-sage (Malaysia), Wild-sage, Red-sage, white-sage (Caribbean), Korsu wire or korsoe wire (Suriname),

Tickberry (South Africa), West Indian Lantana, umbelanterna, put us in Bengal and Gu Phool in Assam, India.

- Genu:- Lantana.
- It is a perennial plant and is toxic to livestock to graze.

• uses:-

- Lantana leaves can display antimicrobial, fungicidal and insecticidal properties.
- L.camara has also been used in traditional herbal medicines for treating a variety of ailments, including cancer, skin itches, leprosy, chicken pox, measles, asthma and ulcers.

#Post -20#

- Study of flowers is called floriculture.
- Telugu name:- Bogada Banthi Puvvu
- English name:- vadamalli, Gomphrena globosa, Makhmali, globe amaranth.

Vadamalli

- Family:- Amaranthaceae.
- Kingdom:- Plantae.
- These are perennial plants.

Chemicals that are present

- Flavonoids.
- Betacyanins.
- Volatiles.
- Mythology:- These are liked a much by the godshiva and kumaraswamy.

  • Uses:-

- In Nepal these are known as Makhmali these are used to make garlands and these garlands are put around arounbrothers'rs necks by their sisters for protection.
- Herbal medicines.

- Used for baby Gripe, cough and diabetes, several respiratory inflammations including asthma, acute and chronic bronchitis, whooping cough, respiratory diseases, jaundice, urinary system and kidney problems.
- Used as supplements in the food industry, cosmetics and livestock.

o Growth conditions:- Heat tolerant and fairly drought resistant.

#POST- 21#

- Telugu name:- Gaddi puvvu.
- English name:- Moss rose.
- Scientific name:- Portulacaceae.

Moss rose

- Family:- Purslane.
- It is used in the treatment of hepatitis, cirrhosis of the liver with ascites, swelling and pain in the pharynx.
- Soil conditions:- Dry soil highlight and warm condition...

#POST- 22#

- Study of flowers is called Floriculture.

- Telugu name:- Adenium.
- English name:- Adenium.
- Commonly known s:- Desert rose, Bangkok kalachuchi and Japanese Frangipani.
- Family:- Apocynaceae.
- Kingdom:- Plantae.
- Uses:- Bonsai plant, Treating wounds, treating the soles of the feet, taking care of skin beauty, relieving pain, treating toothache and treating ulcers.
- Growth conditions:- Temperate regions.
- Taxonomic name:- Adenium obesum.

Adenium

<u>**#POST- 23#**</u>

- Study of flowers is called floriculture.
- Telugu name:- Nandivardhanam.
- English name:- Tabernaemontana divaricata.
- Commonly known as Pinwheel flower, Crape jasmine, East India rosebay and Nero's crown.
- Taxonomic name:- Tabernaemontana divaricata.

Tabernaemontana divaricata

- Family:- Apocynaceae.
- Kingdom:- Plantae.
- Uses:- species is known to produce many alkaloids.

- Growth conditions:- It prefers well-drained sandy loam soil with acidic to neutral pH.
- It grows in tropical and sub-tropical climates where it receives moderate water throughout the year.

#POST- 24#

- Study of birds is called ORNITHOLOGY.
- Chicken - an immature or at least young Bird.
- Telugu name:- Kodi for female, Punju for male.
- Hen For the female name.
- Biddy = A newly hatched chicken.
- Younger male = Cockerel.
- Immature female= Bullet.
- Lifespan = 5 to 10 years.
- Belongs to 2 omnivores.
- Scientific name = Gal Gal domestic service.
- English name = Rooster/Cock (male name).

Rooster/Cock (male name)

-
-

- <u>#POST- 25#</u>

- Telugu name:- Gaddi puvvu.
- English name:- Moss rose.
- Scientific name:- Portulacaceae.

Moss rose

- Family:- Purslane.
- It is used in the treatment of hepatitis, cirrhosis of the liver with ascites, swelling and pain in the thpharynxnx.
- Soil conditions:- dry soil highlight and warm condition...

#POST 26#

- Study of flowers is called floriculture.
- Telugu name:- Nandivardhanam.
- English name:- Tabernaemontana divaricata.

Nandivardhanam

- Commonly known as Pinwheel flower, Crape jasmine, East India rosebay and Nero's crown.
- Taxonomic name:- Tabernaemontana divaricata.
- Family:- Apocynaceae.
- Kingdom:- Plantae.
- Uses:- species is known to produce many alkaloids.
- Growth conditions:- It prefers well-drained sandy loam soil with acidic to neutral pH.
- It grows in tropical and sub-tropical climates where it receives moderate water throughout the year.

#POST 27#

- Study of flowers is called Floriculture.
- Telugu name:- Mandaaram.
- English name:- Hibiscus rosa-Sinensis.
- Taxonomic name:- Hibiscus Rosa-Sinensis.
- Family:- Malvaceae.
- Kingdom:- Plantae.

• Uses:-

- Hair care.
- Shine shoes.
- ph indicator(When used, the flower turns acidic solutions to a dark pink or magenta colour and basic solutions to green).
- Worship.
- Used in Beverages, usually tea.
- Ornamental plant.
- Plantation.
- Decorative purpose.

• National flower

- Several countries and states consider this a National symbol.
- It's a national flower in Malaysia and the unofficial national flower in Haiti.
- Growth conditions:- Tropical and Subtropical regions.

Hibiscus rosa-Sinensis

<u>**#POST- 28#**</u>

- Study of flowers is called Floriculture.
- Telugu name:- Athipathi.
- English name:- Mimosa Pudica .

Touch-me-not

- Commonly known: Sensitive plant, Sleepy plant, Action plant, Touch-me-not, Shame plant.
- Taxonomic name:- Pudica.
- Family:- Fabaceae.
- Kingdom:- Plantae.

Disadvantages:-

- could be a weed for tropical crops.
- It tends to impact corn, coconuts, tomatoes, cotton, coffee etc.
- Dry thickets may result in a fire hazard.
- In addition, Mimosa Pudica can change the physicochemical properties of the soil it invades.
- For example, the total N and K increased significantly In those areas.
- Growth conditions:- tropical and soils with low nutrient concentrations.

<u>**#POST- 29#**</u>

- Study of flowers is called Floriculture.
- English name:- Wedelia acapulcensis.
- Commonly known as Acapulco wedwidely.
- Family:- Asteraceae.

Wedelia acapulcensis

- Kingdom:- Plantae.
- There are around 33,000 species that belong to the same family and are commonly referred to as the sunflower power family.

  • Uses:-

- Cooking oils.
- Food crops.
- Beverages.
- Medicinal (herbal tea and medicinal tea, allergy causes dermatitis).
- Industrial(cola and cigar).
- Ornamental purpose.
- Decorative purpose.

  • Growth conditions:- tropical and warm temperate regions.
• It becomes neutralised in the Mediterranean region.

#POST- 30#

- Study of flowers is called Floriculture.
- Telugu name:- Chitapatakaayala mokka.
- English name:- Ruellia Tuberosa.
- Commonly known:- Minnieroot, feve. root, snapdragon root and sheep potato.
- Taxonomic name:- Ruellia Tuberosa.

Ruellia Tuberosa

- Family:- Acanthaceae.
- Kingdom:- Plantae.
- Uses:- It is believed to be diuretic, anti-diabetic, antipyretic, analgesic, antihypertensive, and gastroprotective, and used for Gonorrhoea.
- It is also used as a natural dye for textiles.
- Growth conditions:- Moist and shady environments and some grasslands flower is something which brings green culture, fragrance, and ornamental purpose and give a pleasant odour. In this blog, I am going to share a few things related to flowers and their features.

#POST 31#

- Study of flowers is called Floriculture.
- Telugu name:- Malle puvvu (malle).
- English name:- Jasmine.
- Taxonomic name:- Jasminum.

Jasmine

- Family: Oleaceae.
- Kingdom:- Plantae.
- Jasminum Fluminense (which is sometimes known by the inaccurate name "Brazilian Jasmine"), Jasminum dichotomum (Gold Coast Jasmine), Jasminum Polyanthum also known as White Jasmine.

- Uses:-

- Fragrance.
- Jasmine tea in china.
- Plantation.
- Decorative purpose.

• National flower

- Several countries and states consider jasmine a National symbol.
- It's a national flower of Syria, Pakistan, Philippines, Indonesia etc.
- City of jasmine:- Damascus.

• Growth conditions:- Tropical and Warm temperate regions.

#POST 32#

- Study of flowers is called Floriculture.
- Telugu name:- Nandivardhanam.
- English name:- Tabernaemontana divaricata.
- Commonly known as Pinwheel flower, Crape jasmine, East India rosebay and Nero's crown.
- Taxonomic name:- Tabernaemontana divaricata.

Nandivardhanam

- Family:- Apocynaceae.
- Kingdom:- Plantae.
- Uses:- species is known to produce many alkaloids.
- Growth conditions:- It prefers well-drained sandy loam soil with acidic to neutral pH.
- It grows in tropical and sub-tropical climates where it receives moderate water throughout the year.

#POST 33#

- Study of flowers is called Floriculture.
- English name:- Sida Rhombifoli.

- Commonly known as Fan petals, Prickly Fan petals, Prickly sida.
- Taxonomic name:- Sida Rhombifolia.

Sida Rhombifolia

- Family:- Malvaceae.
- Kingdom:- Plantae.

- Uses: -

- Sida cordifolia is used to treat Asthma, Tuberculosis, the common cold, flu, headaches, cough and wheezing, urinary tract infections, sore mouth, and fluid retention.

• Growth conditions:- Tropical and subTropical regions.

CHAPTER FIFTEEN

GEOGRAPHY

Part 1

Wah!!!!!!!!!! What a scenic beauty.

I wonder how god would be the foremost experienced person in designing.

I ought to eat what god is eating.

I should follow how God is planning

These are the statements that are flourished in my mind when I am watching the night-blue sky.

That is an astonishing place and it's a feast to my eyes but I wonder how this universe was born.

Whose is the greatest architect in designing this kind of structure around the earth's surface.

Thereafter I walked into my room and asked my parents how the night-blue sky is born.

My parents don't have acumen it's shaped then with my enthusiasm to know every question laid a path to knowing about this universe and night blue sky.

Books are the most beautiful things which give us a path to knowledge. If you believe you are the most intelligent believe me there would be something left that is to be filled within your mind. Books are the most beautiful ever in any life.

If someone is cooking something they would be called a chef then what might be the name of a person who studies these things?

An astronomer

Study /description of the earth is called geography then what is the study of outer space which is having sun, stars, moon, asteroids, etc

Is this universology? My father uttered ??

But after searching I came to know the study of the universe is called cosmology.

Then why do they name cosmology when don't they choose any other option?

How cosmology is derived

It's a Greek word kosmos which means world or outer space then ology means study so cosmology is a study of outer space or universe.

The next question arises in my little mind.

How Does this universe exist? Is this a god creation or any scientific reason or someone holding?

Really, when you question something which you did not have any idea, it gives you many number answers which you had not come across with

Most of the priests say that this universe was created by supernatural power who is omnipresent we can't take it off their words but some do believe this universe is formed due to nebular theory or big bang theory.

Before knowing these concepts let me know what are the elements that are present in our universe.

Galaxy.

What is the galaxy?

Is this a phone?

Nah galaxies are like building blocks of the universe.

Simply universe is formed when a different number of galaxies are combined these galaxies may be regular or irregular.

Again the question arises of what is meant by regular and irregular.

If I don't have an online or oxford dictionary it's going to be the toughest job.

Regular means which is having a definite shape like a rectangle square or triangle

but coming to an irregular it doesn't have any confined shape like regular bodies

what kind of shapes that a regular galaxy has?

They may be elliptical or disc-shaped etc

galaxies are also categorized based on the size of larger galaxies or small galaxies based on the number of stars that are present.

So how many stars are in the small galaxy and large galaxy?

Nearly 1,50,000 or less in small galaxies and large galaxies are having nearly a 5000billion stars.

5000billion stars such a mammoth universe we are having

Realy I don't find 1000 stars in today's view but why?

Maybe they are away from us or have a smaller size

Books have already told me that the universe is filled with a huge number of galaxies which galaxy we are from?

It's the milky way (in Telugu we can call it paalapuntha)

So let us know a few points about our galaxy

Milkyway :

It's like e flat disc shape which is having a bulge at its centre .how big it is around 100000 light-year in s diameter.

Light year!!!!!!!!

What is meant by a light-year?

Sometimes, it is very difficult to calculate long distances

with the help of tape, chain or any other equipment if you try to calculate the astronomical distance with the help of taking which is 3 m long then it would take nearly 10,000 years and it is going to be hereditary work for your family.

To minimize the scale and increase the efficiency light year came into force, it's a unit for length and is used to find the astronomical distance

What is the length of 1 light-year?

Which is equally 9.46×10^15 m

Oh my god it's every fan

What are the main elements present in a milky way?

The Milky way constitutes the solar system.

Solar system Again a new word sol in solar means sun which is derived from the Roman word

Solar means related to the s

Sun, planets, asteroids, meteoroids and dwarf planets are mainly present in the solar system

I know the sun is the star and is present

How many planets are in our solar system?

As per mythology planets can be called Navagraha.

Before 2006 there are 9 planets

They are as follows

- Mercury
- Venus
- Earth
- Mars
- Jupiter
- Saturn
- Uranus
- Neptune
- Pluto

But after 2006 IAU(Indian astronomical unit) considered Pluto as a dwarf planet

But why??

Because it is in the orbit of the Sun and has sufficient mass to attain hydrostatic equilibrium shape if anybody is confined with the above statement then it is called a dwarf planet.

I think my mother is calling for dinner. I am going.

bye-bye.

******after finishing dinner /supper ******

Geography is an interesting topic to learn. let's see what more interesting things are left behind.

Previously, We learnt about the solar system which is having planets, dwarf planets, moons, asteroids, comets and meteors.

We learnt about planets and dwarf planets. what about asteroids, meteors and the moon?

What are asteroids?

These are the tiny particles or the objects which are present in between Mars and Jupiter. These asteroids may sometimes fuse to form heavenly bodies. These are also acted as a segregate objects between inner planets and outer planets

Again what is meant by the inner planet and outer planet?

We shall be discussing this topic in future.

What are meteors?

Meteors are the heavenly bodies that are present in outer space .some of them are mostly present in the mesosphere in the atmosphere .they usually down to the earth's surface due to swift movement due to the friction with air it gets heated up and releases a huge amount of gases into the atmosphere.

What are comets?

These are heavenly bodies that are present in the outer space .they are made up of frozen gases which include water, ammonia, methane and carbon dioxide and a minute amount of hydrogen and helium elements .many comments are present in the solar system and some are beyond pluto. Hailey comet is one of the largest comets as far as our concern

Let us know completely about our planets

There are 4 inner planets and 4 outer planets in our solar system

Inner planets :

- These are also called metallic planets or terrestrial planets.
- Mercury, venus, earth and mass are inner planets.
- They are not far away from the sun.
- Due to solar waves there won't be gas formation on the inner planets.
- These planets don't have rings around them.

Outer planets :

- These are called gases planets.
- Jupiter Saturn, Uranand us, Neptune come under the outer planets.
- These planets are away from the sun.
- As solar waves are not strong to attract these gases they remain in the same position hence they are cal as gases on planets.

- They have rings around the plane.

Complete difference between inner and outer planets
Then another question arises in my mind
Are the physical and geographical features the same or not?
Why is the sun treated separately? anything special?
I got many questions to be answered
Let's see about t sun:-
Sun is a bright star
The most important gases that are present on the surface of the sun are hydrogen and helium
Both hydrogens are Combined to form helium. In this process huge amount of heat is liberated this process is known as nuclear fusion.
the temperature inside the outer region is nearly 6000k
ACTUAL diameter of sun is 13,96,000 km
Another question rises in my mind.
Does the temperature of the sun is constant throughout its body or are there any alterations
Hence we should consider 2 more important statements

- Photosphere.
- Chromosphere.

What is my photosphere?
When dealing with these kinds of questions segregate its word
Photo +sphere
Photo means light
A sphere means an area or space.
It is the outer layer of the sun which emits most of the radiation and light which can be called as visible type
As we have already focused on outer region temperature

when describing the sun
Solar gases are mostly evolved in this region.

What is chromosphere?
Chroma +sphere
Chromo means colour .which is present slight above the photosphere which is thin and shows some colour frequency.

All the planets revolve around the sun in an elliptical orbit means a path on which a planet travels.
Sun is a celestial body which emits heat and light without depending on others.
Planets :
Planets are not celestial bodies because they don't emit heat and light independently but by depending on the light from the sun

<u>**1. mercury (2395 km radius)**</u>

- Hey, I have already come across mercury is this a liquid metal used in a thermometer? Naa!!!!
- In Telugu, it is called buddhi.
- 1st nearest planet close to the sun.
- Distance between mercury and the sun is nearly 57.8 million km the sun.
- The meaning of planet Mercury is the god of commerce and skills.
- Revolution period is 88 days.
- Life is impossino as there is not atmosphere and rapid and cooling temperatures.
- In 1974 MARINA was sent to mercury for information but it acquired very less information.

- But to know the complete details again in 2013 NASA machine was sent on to mercury
- Mass of mercury is about 3.296×1023kg

Are there any satellites for mercury
Mercury has no satellite as it is very close to the sun.

The remaining topics we shall read after some break !!!!!!!!!!!!!!!!!!!!!!!!!!!!

Here comes the second planet
<u>Venus:</u>-

- In Telugu it is called shushakudoi n English it is named after the Roman god called the god of beauty
- Wait !! wait ! here it is given as earth's twin planet but how
- Its diameter is approximately nearer to earth which is 12,106 km.

Features

- The distance between venus and the suna is 107.98million km.
- Hud=ge amount of carbon and methane and other gases are present hence it is not sustainable to live.
- Volcanos are present in mostThe density is 5.24 g/cc.
- It contains a huge number of plateaus, plains and volcanoes.
- No satellite is present.
- It is also called evening star and morning star.
- It is the hottest planet in our solar system which is about 500C.

- Rotates from east to west,t, unlike other planets.
- Rotation 257 days.
- Revolution is about 224.6days.

Earth:-

- In Telugu it is named after the earth goddess bhumi.
- It's the only female name in our solar system.
- Rotation period 23 hours 56 min 4 sec.
- Revolution period is 365.25 days remaining days combined to form a leap year which is having 366days. leap year forms every 4 years.
- Only planet on which sustainability of life exists due to water resources, thermal properties and atmospheric gases.
- Radius of the earth is 6700 km.
- Core region is mainly denser than the upper layers of the earth's surface.
- It is also called a blue planet due to the presence of 71% of water.
- Shape of the earth is geoid.
- Moon is the only natural satellite to our earth.

Mars:-

- 4th nearest planet from the sun and is the last inner planet named after the war.
- It is also called the red planet due to the presence of dust particlesdoesn'tesnt possess any magnetic field.
- Thin atmosphere consists of nitrogen and argon.
- Rotation is about 24.5 hours.
- Revolution period is 687days.

- OLYMPIA is the highest volcano which is even higher than Mount Everest.
- Photos and dominos are the two satellites for mars.
- Temperature ranges from -138 to +138 c.
- Distance between the sun and mars is about 227.3 km.
- Carbon, argon and nitrogen are present in the atmosphere of Mars.

Jupiter:-

- The Largest planet in our solar system which is having a radius of about 69,700 km.
- In Telugu it is called bruhaspathi or garudu.
- Hydrogen, helium and small gases are present on Jupiter.
- No of moons for Jupiter is 67.
- This planet can be seen with our naked eye.
- Having the strongest magnetic force.
- Rotation is about 9.45hours (shortest).
- Jupiter contains 4 huge moons i.e IO, Europa, Ganymede, and Callisto these are called Galileo satsatellitescause of his discovery.
- If Jupiter had become 80 times massive nuclear fusion may take place and becomes the star.
- Mass is about 1.8 X1027Kg.

Saturn:

- 2nd largest planet in our solar system.
- It is named after the Roman god of agriculture.
- It is also called a ringed planet.

- Diameter of this planet is about 60,400 km.
- Distance between the sun and Saturn is about a 1426million km.
- Rings of this planet are made up of ice, dust, and rocks.
- Rotation period is about 10hrs 13 min.
- Saturday is named after Saturn .called the jewel of the solar system.
- It consists mostly of hydrogen and helium like Jupiter.
- Saturn became the 1st planet to have a large number of satellites it's about 87.

Uranus:-

- It is named after the Roman god of the heaven s.
- Diameter of this planet is about 52,080km.
- Distance between the sun and Uranus is about a 2880million km.
- Rotation is about 18 hours and revolution about 84 years.
- It consists of hydrogen and helium gases.
- Major moons Miranda, titania, Oberon, Ariel, Umbriel.
- It rolls from north to south.
- Second least dense planet with 0.68g/cc
- 1st planet to be discovered in modern ages.

Neptune:-

- It is named after the god of the sea.
- It is having a diameter of about 49,520km.
- Distance between the sun and earth is a 4,498million km.

- Rotation of this planet is 19.3 hrs and revolution is about 164.85 years.
- Uranus and Neptune are called twins of the outer planet.
- It consists of mostly hydrogen, helium and methane.
- Consists of nearly 14 satellites.
- Triton is the largest satellite.'

Hence, this is not a complete topic about the gravitational system but a brief description of this universe ...

.**********PART-2*********